Turn Your Computer Into a Money Machine

by Avery Breyer

READ THIS FIRST!

Just to say thank-you for buying my book, I'd like to offer you **FREE access to the Money Machine Inner Circle.**

I think you'll find it insanely useful and you'll get instant access to my special collection of exclusive FREE bonuses:

- A list of the exact tools I use every day (most of which are free to use), which will help you and your "Money Machine" get better results (and THAT tends to lead to getting paid more!)
- A list of the exact services that I used to set up my online business card (my website) quickly and easily, even though I'm not a techie! This is the list I wish I'd had when I set up my first website since it would have saved me a ton of research time — and now it's yours!
- A list of 81 ideas that will be extremely useful as you set up your Money Machine — it's a must-have for anyone who is new to this business!
- Last, but not least, if I ever come across any other info that I think will be of use to you, your membership in the Inner Circle will allow me to get it to you quickly and easily

Ready?

Get your stuff here!

http://averybreyer.com/money-machine-book-opt-in1/

Contents

Introduction

"If you do what you've always done, then you'll get what you've always got." Henry Ford

Could you use a little bit (or maybe a LOT) of extra cash each month? And wouldn't it be great to be able to earn that extra cash without having to get another job? We all know what a mixed blessing an extra job can be, what with the inconvenient hours and the potential for a boss who doesn't care about your need for work-life balance.

Wouldn't it be great if you could earn this extra cash on YOUR terms and:

- Work when you want, and where you want
- Finally have the extra cash you need to afford a few luxuries in your monthly budget
- Take time off whenever you want, without having to beg for permission from your boss and arrange for it weeks or months in advance
- Double, triple, or *quadruple* your hourly wage once you learn to be more efficient at your work, rather than having your boss reward you with more work and zero extra pay

This book will teach you my method for doing all that and more.

"The only point in making money is, you can tell some big shot where to go." Humphrey Bogart

What You'll Learn in This Book

Stick with me and I'll show you how someone with no prior experience in this industry can:

- Use the same process I did to turn my computer into a virtual money machine, earning extra cash whenever I wanted using nothing more than a computer and an internet connection
- Earn hundreds of dollars per month working this business part-time from home, even if you like to work in your pajamas! (I know it's true, because I've done it!)
- Scale this business to the point where you can earn thousands per month and even replace a full-time income
- Set up this business within a week, even if you're not a techie
- Get your first client fast, and many more after that!
- Produce great work that impresses the hell out of your clients and keeps them coming back for more
- Avoid common pitfalls

This book will show you exactly how I managed to make as much as $60 an hour for my time within a couple of months. (And I did this on a part-time basis. I can only imagine how much faster I could have achieved that if I'd put more time into it from the start!)

My Story...

It all started when I joined an online community of people who were all about learning how to earn a living from anywhere in the world, using nothing but their laptops and the internet. That, my friend, is where I first heard about the business model that I'm going to explain to you in this book.

It didn't take long to figure out how to earn more money by being more efficient and finding higher quality clients, and before I knew it, I'd made $60 an hour for my time! All this, despite the fact that I had no formal training in this industry.

I've refined and tweaked this method for maximum effectiveness — and I'm ready to share it all with you.

This method will work from anywhere in the world — from Bali to Boston — as long as you have a computer and a reliable internet connection.

How Much Money Can You Make?

The amount of money you make with this system depends on your work ethic, determination, persistence, and willingness to learn and take action.

For example, some people are happy with earning an extra $500 a month, working a few hours a week in their spare time.

Other people go on to replace their full-time income completely, and earn a few thousand dollars per month with my methods.

How far you want to take this is completely up to you.

The amount of money that your "money machine" makes will depend on your existing skills, and how much you're willing to work. I'm sure I don't need to tell you that the whole "make money online with no effort" thing is a myth, right? Everything requires effort, and this opportunity is no different.

This book isn't about how to start writing books, become a blogger, build websites, start a Multi-Level Marketing business, fill out a bunch of mind-numbing surveys, sell stuff on eBay, or start to harass your friends by trying to sell things to *them*.

This is a much easier business model to get up and running, that can put cash in your pocket a lot sooner than most of those other options, and has little to no start-up costs.

Who Should Read This Book

I am 100% confident that this strategy, which I've used to earn as much as $60 an hour for my time, can help you to earn some extra cash too (and even replace your full-time income!) if you can answer "Yes" to the following questions:

- Do you have a desktop computer or laptop?
- Do you have access to reliable, high-speed internet?
- Are you 100% fluent in the English language?
- Can you read? (Stupid question, I know… you're reading this book, after all. But the point of including this question is to show you just how LOW the barrier to entry is in this industry!)
- Can you string words together into an understandable sentence, in writing?
- Can you write and send an e-mail? (And if not, are you willing to learn?)
- Do you know how to use Google to find information on a topic?
- Are you willing to put in the work to learn the process I'll teach you in this book, and practice until you've mastered it?

This Book is NOT For You If

If you're the kind of person who wants to get rich quick without working for it, then stop now and don't waste your time reading this book. I can't teach you how to get rich quick with no work. The bottom line is that while it's possible to start making money quickly with this business model, it's not an overnight ticket to riches and wealth.

If you're the kind of person who is impatient and gives up easily, then you too, shouldn't bother reading further. While some people will implement the strategies outlined in this book and start making money within a week, for others, it will take longer. To maximize your odds of succeeding at this, you've got to be in it for the long haul.

Never Give Up

I say that a lot. But it's because I believe it 100%.

I've been playing around with various ways to make money online while working from home for years.

The thousands of dollars I've spent on books and training courses have helped me to find the ways of earning extra cash that actually work for me. And of course, I've also spent a lot of time and money learning about other methods that, as it turned out, were not a good fit for me after all. But there was no way of knowing that without jumping in and learning everything I could about it first.

If I'd quit after the first thing I tried that didn't work out, I wouldn't be where I am today. If you'd quit after the first thing you tried, you wouldn't be here either. (So kudos to you for not giving up!)

The point is, you've got to invest your time and money (as you did by buying this book!), you can't give up, and you've got to experiment if you want to figure out a way of earning the cash you need to fund the lifestyle you want.

The method I'm going to teach you in this book allowed me to earn several hundred dollars in my first month, working extremely part-time hours.

By the end of two months, I was able to figure out how to earn as much as $60 per hour by doing this.

Out of all the methods I've used in an attempt to earn a buck online, this method led to the fastest results, and made the most money for my time.

My Promise to You

I promise you that I'm going to share with you everything that you need to know to get this business up and running.

Like I said, it'll take some work on your part to get this thing going, but once you do, it's like a money tap that you can turn on and off at will.

And if after reading through this book, you want some extra support with putting the pieces together in a way that works for you, join my Money Machine Inner Circle (it's FREE!) and I'll show you where to get it.

http://averybreyer.com/money-machine-book-opt-in1/

Don't be the kind of person who is a dreamer of big dreams, but stops short at taking action.

Be the kind of person who takes control, makes plans, and takes *massive* action. That is how you get onto the road to success.

The strategies you'll learn in this book will show you how to turn your computer into a money machine, just like I did. All you need to do to learn how is keep reading.

How I Turned My Computer Into a Money Machine

"Making money is art and working is art and good business is the best art." Andy Warhol

Alright, let's cut to the chase. You want to know how I turned my computer into a money machine, and I'm going to tell you! This chapter will give you the 10,000 foot view of how my system works and what you can attain if you follow in my virtual footsteps.

Basically, what I'm going to do is teach you how to earn money with a very specific type of freelance writing that is in extremely high demand. And don't worry, this kind of writing isn't particularly tricky to do once you know the right formula to follow and how to find people who will pay you for doing it.

Now, at first glance, getting into freelance writing sounds intimidating... especially if you're not already a writer with a fancy degree in journalism.

But over and over again, I've been able to earn extra money using this method. And I am 100% confident that you can learn to do the same.

(And nope, I most certainly do not have a degree in journalism, fancy, or otherwise.)

Back when I first found out about this opportunity, I was floored when I realized that I could easily earn anywhere from $20 to $60 an hour writing simple articles in my spare time, even though I was new to this industry.

This was before I'd ever written a single book. This was back when I'd never earned so much as a single dime writing for anyone else.

What Kind of Writing Is This?

Don't worry, I'm not suggesting something crazy like trying to write for *The New York Times*.

Nope. The kind of writing I'm talking about is extremely low stress, no pressure kind of stuff.

The specific kind of writing jobs I'm going to teach you to get are SEO Writing jobs.

SEO Writing — What Is That?

SEO is an acronym for Search Engine Optimization.

On the internet, Google is king of the search engines. According to SearchEngineLand and figures obtained from comScore, Google is by far the most widely used search engine in the entire world. It's used countless times per day to find information on an enormous range of topics.

http://searchengineland.com/google-worlds-most-popular-search-engine-148089

And this is good news for you, the aspiring freelance writer.

Website owners need people to write search-engine-friendly, informative content that is written in a way that maximizes the chances that it'll be found by people who use search engines like Google to find information.

And what you're going to be doing is writing short articles (usually around 500 words or so), for their websites. Generally, these will be small business websites. You'll find demand for writing in a wide variety of niches, everything from pest removal to wedding supplies.

This, my friend, is SEO writing. The barrier to entry is low, plus most people have never heard of it — these factors make it relatively easy for a newcomer, with no experience, to break into the industry.

SEO writing may sound intimidating — after all, most people have never heard of the term SEO, never mind trying to write with it in mind.

But don't be intimidated. All it is, is writing about a topic from scratch — usually around 500 words — and ensuring that said content is packed full of useful, accurate information. The client will tell you what they want the article to be about. All you have to do is research the topic online and put together an article about it.

So what makes SEO writing different from writing regular articles? The client will often give you a keyword or phrase (for example, "Get Rid of Raccoons") that you'll have to sprinkle throughout the article, paying particular attention to include it in the headlines and sub-headlines.

How I Tripled My Hourly Earnings from $20 to $60 Per Hour with SEO Writing

I'm sharing these numbers with you in the hopes that you'll get as excited as I am by the possibilities that await you with this kind of writing business.

But first, let me explain the reasons for the large swing in hourly wage…

When I was first getting started I needed to get my feet wet and build my confidence. So I'd write for anyone, at any price. I wanted to get a feel for what would be expected of me, without the pressure of knowing they'd agreed to pay me a large amount of money.

But even so, less than three weeks after starting this new venture, when I found myself making $20 an hour as I worked in my pajamas on the couch, or from the lounger beside the swimming pool, I figured this was not half bad. Especially since I had no prior experience in being a freelance writer.

And keep in mind, the U.S. Federal Minimum Wage for most workers is only $7.25 an hour. Yet there I was, a newbie writer-for-hire, and I was making almost triple that!

And If You Don't Want to Write So Much…

When I'd been at this for five weeks or so, I was struck by the urge to experiment. So I outsourced the writing to freelancers that I found on oDesk.com (now known as UpWork.com). I was pleased to see that I ended up making a decent profit for my time after paying my writers.

Why not?! I was curious whether or not I could earn more money per hour of my time this way.

What do I mean by outsourcing?

I hired other ghostwriters to do my writing for me — that way, all I had to do before turning in an article to a client was to give it a quick proofread.

Depending on what you pay your writers, and how much time you need to put into editing and proofreading their work, this can be a profitable way to take a break from the bulk of the writing.

And if you're a slow writer, you may find that you make more money per hour when outsourcing the writing (only leaving the final proofread for you to do yourself), compared to writing every single word on your own.

For example, say you're a slow typist and it takes you one hour to write a $20 article.

What if you outsourced the writing to someone else who, because they can bang out two articles per hour, is happy with $10 per article? You'd pocket the $10 profit between what you're paying them and what your client is paying you.

If it takes you 15 minutes to check over each one of their completed articles (proofreading, plagiarism check etc.), you'd be able to get through four articles in an hour, increasing your effective hourly wage from $20 an hour for doing it all yourself, to $40 an hour by outsourcing the writing.

And don't worry, you don't even have to hide the fact that you're doing this. As far as my writers were concerned, they were ghostwriting for my writing agency, knowing full-well that their work was being sent off to another client afterwards. And my clients knew that I was outsourcing the writing — all they cared about was that the finished product that I provided them with was good.

Feeling guilty about the thought of making more money per hour than your writers?

Don't. In addition to the fact that you're spending time on proofreading their work, you are also saving your writers the time and effort of communicating with the clients and *finding* those clients in the first place — that's worth something.

Finding Premium SEO Writing Clients

After those early successes I began looking for premium clients — the ones who had deeper pockets and could afford to pay higher prices for my work. That's when I hit gold — and reached an earnings milestone of $60 per hour for my time.

Sure, no-one is going to buy a private jet and fly off into the sunset with that, but it's a hell of a lot better than what the average second job will pay, right?

The first time I managed to pull off $60 an hour was when I was asked to write a batch of articles on a topic that I was very familiar with, and could write them up without needing to do any research. I whipped up three articles of 500 words apiece in an hour, and was paid $20 per article.

Now I'm a pretty quick typist (and you will be too, if you follow all of the advice in this book!) — but even if you're only half as quick as I am, in the previous example you'd have ended up making $30 per hour of your time... that's still not half bad, and is more than FOUR times higher than the federal minimum wage!

Later on, I decided to increase my rates and see if I could land some clients at these new, higher rates. Lo and behold, I was able to pull off a rate of $30 for 500 words now. Because I was getting paid better, I had to make sure that these articles were better than the el cheapo ones I'd started out with in the beginning. So I spent a whopping 30 minutes per article now, and again, made $60 per hour.

Now remember — these articles are NOT expected to be full of pizazz, personality and pop! (If you can add that in, and still make it worth your time, more power to you. I'm just pointing out that it's not *required* for this level of client.) You're not writing for a high traffic website with high expectations, such as the *Huffington Post*.

Nope, these articles are likely going to be for websites that you've never heard of — websites owned by small business owners who don't have the time or desire to write content themselves, don't have the budget for a high-end writer, but need to fill out their website with a few articles here and there. All that you're being paid to do is to write a functional article that is useful, written from scratch, and is free of errors (well, as free as humanly possible, anyhow.)

However, once you gain more experience, and improve your writing skills, you can go after significantly higher paying writing jobs.

But remember, the purpose of *this* book is to teach you how to get started as a total newbie to freelance writing. Unless you're already a very talented writer, you're better off working on improving your skills before you pursue the higher-priced jobs. The last thing you want to do is jump into offering premium writing services before you've improved your writing chops enough, and end up disappointing your clients. This is why SEO writing is the perfect way to earn money and improve your skills at the same time — SEO writing clients will not expect the world from you, all they want is functional articles that are free of errors. No pressure stuff... really!

Anyhow, I truly believe that you can learn to do all of this too. You've just got to know how to start, what kind of writing jobs to pursue, and where to find them. After that, the sky's the limit.

It becomes kind of like a money tap, that you can turn on and off at will.

Need more money? Bang out a few articles and you've got it. Need a break? You're in charge, take one!

Can You Really Do This?

Assuming you're a native English speaker (or fluent enough to pass as one) who can read and write, you can do this.

For real.

If you've ever written an e-mail to a friend, you can obviously write, so that settles that.

You're *reading* this book right now, so that settles THAT requirement too.

And, well, the Native English Speaker requirement is something only you know whether or not you meet.

What is a Native English Speaker? For the purposes of this kind of writing work, it means someone who has used English as their primary means of communication since early childhood. That experience gives you a really good eye for the language and you'll intuitively know if something "looks right" on the page. Alternatively, if English is your second language, you'll have the best chance of getting SEO writing jobs if your English writing skills are as good as those of a native speaker.

Sure, you're not perfect, no-one is — but using English extensively for so many years gives you a leg up on the competition.

Those are the most important qualities to have right now — the rest can be learned with a bit of time, practice, and the right instruction. You'll get the instruction you need here in this book. And the practice is up to you.

But Wait, What if I Suck at Writing?

Look, don't worry about it. Odds are, you only think you suck at writing because back in your school days you weren't the greatest at writing formal essays and research reports.

But this kind of writing is completely different.

SEO writing is much less formal.

It's the kind of stuff that even someone who royally sucked at writing back in their school days can learn to master. I've seen all kinds of people learn to write excellent content, even people who used to get C's in English Language Arts.

Writing is like a muscle, the more you use it, the stronger it gets.

So remember, just because you used to suck at writing doesn't mean you're destined to stay that way. With the right instruction and practice, you are perfectly capable of becoming more than good enough to write SEO content!

Summing Up

The main problem that most people run into as they try to get into this line of work is that they just don't know where to start. So they quit, and go back to life as they were living it before.

This book will help to ensure that you don't fall into that trap.

There is more than enough information in this book to get going — even if you're totally new to this industry.

But before we dive deep into the how-to stuff, I'm going to show you some of the benefits you can experience from jumping into this line of work. Because having a clear idea of what you can gain from doing this will make it much easier to maintain the motivation and focus you'll need to succeed at this.

6 Reasons Why You'll Love This Method of Making a Buck

"I have ways of making money that you know nothing of." John D. Rockefeller

Now that you know that you are perfectly qualified for SEO writing, I want to share with you some of the advantages of earning money in this manner. And there are many. Here are five of the biggest reasons why people love this business model.

1. You have potential for high earnings.

The beauty of this system is that it can allow you to earn an extremely good hourly wage for your time. When I first started out, I averaged about $20 per hour for my time. However, within a few months, I was averaging around $35-$40 per hour, and sometimes hitting spikes of $60 per hour. A year later, I was almost always making $50-60 per hour of my time.

There are several reasons for the quick increase in hourly wage.

Your hourly wage is based largely on how quickly you can bang out an article. If you're getting paid $15 for a 500-word article, and it takes you one hour to get it done, then you've made $15 per hour, working from home, in your pajamas if you want to!

However, the more you do this, the faster you'll get at researching, writing, and editing your articles. After a while, you may find yourself finishing a 500-word article in 20 minutes — do three of those in an hour and BOOM! You just made $45 an hour.

(Don't worry about your typing speed... none of us are born as speed-typists after all. However, that can be fixed with a bit of time and effort. If you sign up for the Money Machine Inner Circle (it's FREE), I'll provide you with a list of my favorite resources, including a free online typing class that will teach you how to improve your typing in the exact same way that I learned to type many years ago!)

But believe me, if you continue to improve your writing skills (and you will, right?), you can do better than $15 per 500 word article.

Here's an example of a client who is offering $20 per 500 words (4 cents per word) to **freshen up** an article, $25 per 500 words (5 cents per word) for a **new** SEO article, and as much as $40 per 500 words (8 cents per word) for web copy.

I did some work for this individual, and was paid as agreed upon.

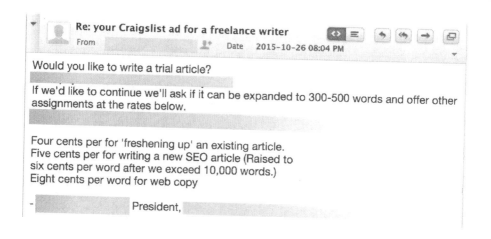

Re: your Craigslist ad for a freelance writer
From ▓▓▓▓▓▓▓▓ Date 2015-10-26 08:04 PM

Would you like to write a trial article?

If we'd like to continue we'll ask if it can be expanded to 300-500 words and offer other assignments at the rates below.

Four cents per for 'freshening up' an existing article.
Five cents per for writing a new SEO article (Raised to six cents per word after we exceed 10,000 words.)
Eight cents per word for web copy

- ▓▓▓▓▓▓   President, ▓▓▓▓▓▓▓▓▓▓▓▓

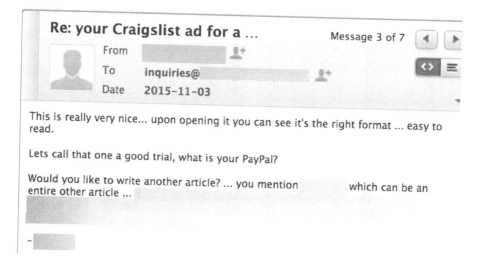

Re: your Craigslist ad for a ...   Message 3 of 7

From ▓▓▓▓▓▓▓▓
To   inquiries@▓▓▓▓▓▓▓▓▓▓
Date 2015-11-03

This is really very nice... upon opening it you can see it's the right format ... easy to read.

Lets call that one a good trial, what is your PayPal?

Would you like to write another article? ... you mention ▓▓▓▓▓ which can be an entire other article ... ▓▓▓▓▓▓▓▓▓▓

- ▓▓▓▓▓

(The screenshots of our e-mail correspondence are slightly different in appearance because I was using two different e-mail accounts at the time…)

Anyhow, the longer you do this, the better you'll be at finding higher paying clients.

First of all, you'll have more experience and feel more confident about asking for higher prices.

Secondly, the more writing you do, the better your work will be, and that alone will justify higher prices for your work. Soon, you could be getting paid $20 for a 500-word article. And if you're still able to bang out three of those in an hour, you'll make $60 per hour of your time.

And later still, you can find clients who will pay you $30 for a 500-word article — that will allow you to spend a bit more time on each article, say 30 minutes, and still earn $60 an hour.

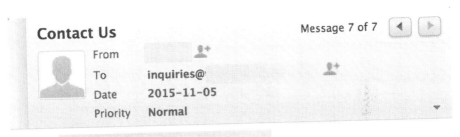

At these rates, you can see how you wouldn't need to write that many articles per working day to end up making a few thousand dollars per month. For example, if you make $30 per article, and write 5 of them per day, 5 days a week, and it takes you only 30 minutes to finish each *one, that's 2.5 hours of work per working day to bring home an extra $3000 per month.*

Say you don't need $3000 per month — then work less. You could do 2 articles per day, 5 days per week, and bring home an extra $1200 per month, working only an hour per working day.

Bring on as many clients as you need to reach your income goals.

Even if all you can do is write a single $30 article in an hour, you'll be making more than four times the federal minimum wage — not half bad at all if you ask me!

A Look into the Future

The longer you keep at this, the more likely it is that your writing will improve to the point where you can branch out into higher paying work, including writing for blogs that pay $50 or even over $100 or more per 500-word post!

But don't take my word for it. If you do a simple Google search for "blogs that pay $100 an article," you'll see lots of options come up.

Once you really know what you're doing, you can move past the people who want nothing more than low-budget articles for the search engines. You can start to pursue clients who are have more sophisticated needs. Often, they sell products that are expensive and quite complex. These types of clients need to explain what they're selling in a way that gets people excited about it and itching to buy — they need writers who can provide regular, informative blog posts that will help them to build their e-mail list, establish them as an authority in their field, and attract new customers.

For clients like these, $100 per 500-word blog post is a pittance and they won't blink when you quote your rates.

Obviously this kind of thing isn't something you'll pursue from the start, but I wanted you to know what's out there so you can start thinking about where you might be able to take your writing business over the long-term.

This higher paying work can be more fun to do, and you'll be less rushed when producing content.

2. Most people have never heard of it, so there's less competition.

I bet that if you ask your circle of friends if they've ever heard of SEO writing, they'll give you a quick "Nope!"

The fact that there is an extremely high demand for SEO writers, most freelance writers are unfamiliar with the ins and outs of SEO, and the average person doesn't know that this specific kind of work even exists, means there is not that much REAL competition for work.

What is REAL competition? The people who actually know what they're doing.

And believe me, if you talk to a few people who have tried to hire SEO writers, you'll hear again and again that most of the people they've hired didn't work out because they weren't very good at it.

You're going to be different though.

You're reading this book and learning what you need to know to be one of the few who actually knows what they're doing.

This makes getting your foot in the door pretty easy.

And don't worry if you're not familiar with SEO now. This book will give you an overview of what makes SEO writing different from regular freelance writing — believe me, it's not complicated — which will give you a huge edge over those who have no idea.

3. The demand for writers is expected to grow.

According to the United States Department of Labor, the demand for writers is going to grow over the next several years. So taking into account the fact that there should be more writing jobs in future, not less, and the fact that SEO writing isn't on most people's radar, you have good odds of finding work (especially if you follow my system).

I know that my system works in today's market — I've been testing it right up until the date that this book was published (in fact, I landed 4 new clients in the 2 weeks leading up to this book's publication date!) There's no way I was going to publish this book without being 100% certain that my methods for finding clients work right NOW.

And in case you're wondering…

I do all of my freelance work under another business name that has nothing to do with "author Avery Breyer."

So it's not as though I'm able to convince clients to hire me by saying "I'm best-selling author Avery Breyer." As far as my clients are concerned, I'm just another random freelancer… just like you're going to be!

4. You can set your own hours, and work wherever you like.

Wouldn't it be fantastic to be able to work WHENever you want, and WHEREever you want?

SEO writing allows you to do that. My clients are primarily located in North America, and I've written articles for them anywhere from typical North American suburbia to Bali. I've written my articles in coffee shops like Starbucks, sitting by an infinity swimming pool in Malaysia, and enjoying the ocean view in Hawaii. Other times my "office" for writing is less interesting — sitting in my pajamas in bed.

The point is, you really can do this pretty much anywhere, as long as you'll have access to a computer and reliable wifi.

Your hours of work will be whatever suits you. If you like to get up bright and early and finish your work early in the day, you can do that. If you're a parent who's home with your kids all day, you can squeeze in an article here, an article there… whenever you have a few minutes to spare. Or maybe you're a night owl, and you'd rather put off your work until the evening, allowing you to do other things during daylight hours. When you work is completely up to you.

5. SEO writing is easy to learn.

As I've said before, it really is very easy to learn this industry, and I'll go over everything you need to know in order to get started in this book.

Even if you think your typing skills royally suck, and that's holding you back from trying this, you can learn to type for FREE online. Stick with your online typing lessons for a while and you'll be typing at a respectable speed in no time… and be able to write articles faster, and make more money per hour.

If you haven't done so already, sign up for the Money Machine Inner Circle using the link below (it's FREE!) and you'll get access to a FREE report that lists my recommended FREE typing tutorials, plus a list of the exact tools that I use every day in my writing business. Why waste time spinning your wheels trying to figure out what tools to use when you can have it all laid out for you?

http://averybreyer.com/money-machine-book-opt-in1/

6. You don't have to be good with technology.

Honestly, it's ridiculously easy to master what you need to know in order to get going. In its simplest form, all you need to get started is an e-mail account, a computer or laptop, and internet access.

If you want to get more sophisticated, you can set up a website to advertise your services. Although it's not absolutely necessary, I highly recommend it. Don't let inexperience put you off doing this either — nowadays, it's easy for even non-techies to set up a simple website. I'll discuss this topic a bit more later in the book.

Action Step

If you're a "hunt and peck" one or two-fingered typist, then you need to learn to type faster. And no, faster hunting and pecking won't do. You need to learn to type for real. You know, fingers on the keyboard, staring at your computer screen not the keyboard.

Or maybe you can kind of type for real, but you're really slow.

If either of the above two scenarios applies to you, I highly recommend that you commit to practicing your typing skills for 15-30 minutes every day, starting now.

Forgive me for repeating this again, but remember, if you sign up for the Money Machine Inner Circle (it's free!) via the link beneath reason #5, I'll give you a list of resources which includes a link to a website that offers free typing lessons. Take advantage of this. You'll be amazed at how much you've improved after only a few weeks of practice.

The faster you type, the more money you'll make per hour of your time.

Summing Up

With the high potential for earnings, lack of major competition, ability to work when and how you like, easy learning curve, and minimal technology required, this is an attractive way to earn a buck. Now that you understand some of the perks of getting into this business, it's time to learn some of the insider's lingo that you'll come across. The next chapter will go over that in detail.

Insider's Lingo That You've Got to Understand

"I used to go away for weeks in a state of confusion." Albert Einstein

Every industry has its lingo… you know, that gobbledegook that only those "in the know" understand.

If you want to become a successful freelance SEO writer, you need to understand the insider's lingo.

But don't let that worry you.

After a quick read of this chapter you'll have it all down. Honestly, it's not that difficult to understand, and if you've spent any time surfing the internet, you've probably come across this stuff without even realizing it.

Ready? Here we go then!

The Lingo

Here are a few important terms that you need to be familiar with. Don't worry if you don't have them memorized after your first read. All you really need is to have an idea of what they mean, and the ability to come back here to refresh your memory at a later date if necessary.

The Keyword Phrase

The keyword phrase (often simply called the "keyword"), refers to the word or combination of words that internet searches use to find information with the search engines. So you know how you have to enter some text into Google when you do a search for information? Every time you do this, you've used a keyword phrase.

Most of your clients will tell you what keyword phrase they want the article to focus on, and if they don't tell you, then be sure to ask them.

It's rare to be asked to use a single word as your keyword phrase. This is because single words are too difficult to rank highly for in the search results. Instead, most SEO companies go after keyword phrases that are several words long, since there is less competition for rankings.

For example, an article about do-it-yourself home maintenance might be targeting people who use search engines like Google to find information on the search term, "DIY Home Maintenance." If a client asked you to include that keyword in the article, you'd simply make sure to include the phrase "DIY Home Maintenance" (don't include the quotes) in the article's headline, plus a few more times in the content of your article.

Often, clients will ask you to use a particular keyword phrase as the anchor text for a link to another internet webpage that you include in the article.

Links

Links are the (usually) underlined text in a webpage, eBook, or PDF that you click on to be taken to a particular webpage.

Anchor Text

See this link to Google? (I know you can't "click" on a link in a book, so just imagine that "link to Google" is on a webpage, ok?) The underlined text that you click on to be taken to another webpage is called the anchor text. So in this example, the link's anchor text is "link to Google."

Whenever you use anchor text to link to a webpage from your article, be sure that the anchor text is related to the topic of the webpage being linked to.

For example, if you're writing an SEO article on the topic of rainbows, and you use the anchor text "biggest rainbow ever seen," then ensure that if a reader clicks on that link, they will end up on a webpage that is about the biggest rainbow ever seen. Do not use anchor text "biggest rainbow ever seen" to link to a page about how to get a deal when buying a house — this would lead to a bad reader experience for anyone who comes across your article (because your link made them think it would take them to a page about the biggest rainbow, not buying a house) — and your client will not be happy either.

Popular writing software, such as Microsoft Word and OpenOffice, all give you the ability to add what they call a "hyperlink" to your article. This is the function you'll use to add your anchor text and links within your articles.

Internet Browser

An internet browser is the program that you use to view websites on the internet. Common internet browsers include Firefox, Chrome, and Safari.

URL

The only thing you need to know about this term is that a URL is the website address that appears in your search engine's address bar. An example of a URL is: https://www.wikipedia.org.

Webpage

Whenever you surf the internet, you're looking at a webpage in your internet browser. The webpage may contain text, links, images, videos, and other content.

Summing Up

See? The lingo is not too bad. And remember, if a client ever asks you about something you aren't sure of, you can always Google it to find out more. And if further clarification is needed for any lingo mentioned by your client, don't hesitate to send them an e-mail to ask questions.

In the next chapter we're going to get into writing tips. Because you can't start building your SEO writing business unless you understand how to write content that's intended for internet users. But don't worry — with a bit of practice, you'll see that it's not very hard at all.

7 Secrets That You Need to Know to Succeed

"Life is really simple, but we insist on making it complicated." Confucius

If you're going to succeed at earning money via SEO writing, you need to throw out almost everything you learned about writing in high school or college.

Back then, you might have been told things such as "when writing a paragraph, the first sentence should introduce the paragraph topic, the middle sentences should discuss the topic introduced in the first sentence, and the final sentence should sum up the entire paragraph."

Yeah, well, that may have pleased your high school English teacher or college professor, but it'll put impatient internet searchers to sleep. And cause you to lose clients.

Writing content for the internet is completely different — and I'm going to show you the right way to do it. Here are the 7 secrets of being successful at writing a good SEO article.

1. Do Not Write Long Paragraphs

Remember those long flowing paragraphs that you were encouraged to create for your school essays? Never again. Do not, for the love of Pete, do that for your SEO articles.

Instead, aim to make each paragraph no more than four sentences.

See? The first paragraph I wrote in this section had two sentences, while the second paragraph had only one sentence. That's the style you ought to be aiming for in everything you produce for your SEO writing clients.

Your goal should be to make your SEO articles as easy to read as possible. And what's easier to read? A few lines of text at a time? Or a paragraph that goes on and on like this one will? Paragraphs that are long tend to be skipped over, or readers give up on them part way through because they get tired of the effort required to continue on. In fact, I'll be shocked if you're still reading this paragraph right now. It's just too long. Are you really still here? If so, you're one hell of a trouper! Anyhow, these articles are not going to be read by your high school teacher or college professor, whose life mission is to turn you into a good scholar. No. These articles are going to be read by busy internet searchers who have a world of information at their fingertips, accessible in seconds. If your article is boring and rambles on and on and on, or if your article is difficult to read because of all the super long paragraphs you've included, those internet searchers will hit the back button on their web browser so fast that it'll make your head spin. Then they'll go to some other website for their information — a website with content that's easier to read. And your client will not be pleased.

Got it? Ok, onwards then.

2. Use Sub-Headlines To Break Up the Text

According to a study by Jakob Nielson (please see the URL below), most people who search for information online tend to just scan the articles that come up in search results, rather than read every word.

http://www.nngroup.com/articles/how-users-read-on-the-web/

I know.

That's depressing to hear when you've just gone and written 500 words of spectacularly useful information on your client's topic.

But don't despair.

Because one great way to draw fickle readers in is with magnetic sub-headlines that pull them deeper into the text. And at the very least, if you do it right, they'll at least stick with the article to the end by skimming your sub-headlines.

Expert Tip: Remember those keywords we talked about back in the chapter about Insider's Lingo? If you really want to impress your client, include the target keyword a few times in the article's sub-headlines. Obviously, if for some reason your client doesn't want you to do it, don't. But most clients will love you for it!

3. Write Short Sentences

Most people find shorter sentences easier to understand and follow along with. Combine that with the short attention span of most internet searchers, and there's a compelling case to be made for keeping it short and sweet.

Here is an example of what not to do:

"Many people all over the world enjoy having dogs, which happen to be magnificent creatures, as pets because they are incredibly loyal, very cute, and are fun to have around."

And here is what you should do instead:

"Many people all over the world enjoy having dogs as pets. These magnificent creatures are loyal, very cute, and fun to have around."

The second version is much easier to follow due to the shorter sentence length. Yet it still includes all of the information that the writer tried to incorporate in the first example. Try to emulate the shorter sentence length of the second example when you write for SEO clients.

4. ~~Eliminate Words That Are Unnecessary~~
4. Eliminate Unnecessary Words

This helps to keep your writing short and punchy. It also makes your writing easier for readers to follow.

For example, take a look at the following two sentences.

"It is commonly accepted as a fact that dogs are a man's best friend in the whole wide world."

"Dogs are man's best friend."

The first sentence is awkward and wordy. These are not desirable traits for online content.

The second sentence is much improved because I removed the extra words that were cluttering up the original.

Granted, if you eliminate excess words from your sentences, you'll have to work harder to reach your minimum word counts. However, this extra time should more than be covered by the fact that your attention to providing clients with articles that are not padded with unnecessary words will lead to more repeat business (i.e., less time spent on your part hustling to find new clients).

5. Make Your Meaning Obvious — This is Not the Time to be Clever

Don't use obscure references in an attempt to show how clever you are — it's going to backfire because most people will be too impatient to try and figure out what you mean.

You see, the trick to writing effective online content is to make it easy for readers to get through it quickly without having to think too hard.

Generally speaking, you should use simple words that pretty much anyone will be familiar with. Here's an example of the kind of choices you'll face.

"Snow is ubiquitous in January."
 versus
"Snow is everywhere in January."

If you have a choice between using the word "ubiquitous" or "everywhere," please choose everywhere. There are too many people who won't know what ubiquitous means, so there's no benefit to using it.

6. Write in the Active Voice

Whenever possible, write in the active voice. This will make your writing easier to understand and less boring. And let's face it, submitting boring articles to your client won't make them happy, right?

Take a look at the following two phrases.

"Sarah ate the whole cake." (Active voice)

"The whole cake was eaten by Sarah." (Passive voice)

Here's another example.

"The boy loves clowns." (Active voice)

"Clowns are loved by the boy." (Passive voice)

Do you notice the differences between the active and passive voice in the above examples?

You can read more about the active versus passive voice here:

http://www.towson.edu/ows/activepass.htm

Take some time and write out a few sentences in the active voice. Then write them out in the passive voice for comparison. Do you notice that the sentences written in the active voice not only sound better, but are easier to understand? Plus, they get the point across in fewer words, which is always a good thing for content that'll be read online.

7. Put Your Keyword in the Right Places

Ok, so what is considered the "right place" and "right frequency" for keyword usage will vary from client to client. Some tend to be very aggressive with keyword usage, and others are less so. However, here are some rules of thumb to follow for a typical 500 word article. Make adjustments based on your client's individual preferences.

I) Always include the keyword in the article's headline.

II) Always include the keyword in the last sub-headline of the article.

III) Use the keyword in one or two of the other sub-headlines of the article too, if you can do it without making the article read awkwardly.

IV) Write down some synonyms for the keyword and sprinkle those throughout the article.

V) Use the keyword in the first sentence of the article.

Bonus Tip: Do Not, For the Love of Pete, Commit Plagiarism

In a nutshell, plagiarism refers to copying someone else's work and not giving them credit. It should be obvious not to do this, but if you do some extra research about writing SEO articles online, you might come across some shady characters who advocate this kind of nonsense.

Here are some examples of what NOT to do when writing SEO articles for your clients:

- Copying another article that you found on the internet word-for-word
- Copying another article that you found on the internet, but changing the order of the sentences to make it different
- Copying another article that you found on the internet, but substituting synonyms for a bunch of the words in an attempt to hide the fact that you copied the other article

You can read more about plagiarism here:

http://www.lib.sfu.ca/help/academic-integrity/plagiarism

If you copy someone else's work, it's plagiarism, plain and simple. Your client will have tools to catch this sort of thing and it'll be your quick ticket out of business if you try it.

Keep in mind that you don't have to give anyone credit for information that is common knowledge. For example, most people are aware that Michigan is part of the United States, right? So if you were writing an article and mentioned that Michigan is located in the United States, you don't have to give anyone else credit for that information, even if that information appears in many other articles online or elsewhere.

Summing Up

Now that you're armed with some writing tips to make your work really stand out from the competition, it's time to learn about some of the more common writing pitfalls, and how to avoid them.

In the next chapter, I'm going to share with you my cheat sheet for this — it will help you to produce higher quality work that commands higher prices and leads to more cash lining your pocket!

My Cheat Sheet For Avoiding Common Pitfalls

"No, we don't cheat. And even if we did, I'd never tell you." Tommy Lasorda

There are tons of ways to screw up the written English language, and this cheat sheet is your ticket to avoiding the errors most likely to be noticed by your clients. Always proofread your work with the following potential mistakes in mind.

And don't worry if grammar wasn't your strongest subject in school. There are many ways of explaining the errors in this list, and for most of them, I've been able to avoid using an overly technical grammarian explanation and instead, have used simple, easy-to-remember explanations.

1. "Its" versus "It's"

"It's" should only be used if substituting the words "it is" would make sense. If not, then "its" is the correct choice.

For example, "It's a delicious cake" can also be written as "It is a delicious cake"; therefore, you can use "it's" if you want.

On the other hand, if you were writing "Its roof was in a horrible state," you should leave out the apostrophe since "It is roof was in a horrible state" doesn't make sense.

2. "Your" versus "You're"

"You're" should only be used if substituting the words "you are" would make sense. If not, then "your" is the correct choice.

For example, "You're right about the weather being beautiful" can also be written as "You are right about the weather being beautiful." So go ahead and use either "you're" or "you are."

On the other hand, if you were writing "Your shirt is missing a button," changing it to "You are shirt is missing a button" makes zero sense; therefore, you cannot substitute "you're" for "your" and "You're shirt is missing a button" would be incorrect.

3. "To" versus "Too" versus "Two"

Let's get started with the easiest of the three. "Two" should only be used if you are referring to the number "2."

- "There are two apples left in the fridge."
- "Two couples will be joining us for dinner."

"Too" should only be used if substituting "also" or "excessively" would make sense. Examples of correct usage include the following:

- "I want to read that book too." ("I want to read that book also.")

- "There is too much salt in this salad." ("There is excessive salt in this salad.")
- "The wall color is too dark." ("The wall color is excessively dark.")

Pretty much every other situation requires the use of the word "to." Here are some examples (you'll notice that for none of them would the number "2," or the words "also" or "excessively," make sense):

- "That shirt belongs to Pete."
- "I am going to the mall."
- "He went to the car dealership."
- "I want to draw."
- "He does not want to work."
- "Do you want to help?"

4. "There" versus "Their" versus "They're"

"They're" should only be used if substituting "they are" would make sense. Here are some examples of the correct use of "they're":

- "They're a great company to work for."
- "They're a fun group of people to hang out with."

"Their" should only be used if you are trying to indicate possession of some sort (and not the supernatural kind!) Here are some examples of the correct use of "their":

- "I had a great time at their party."
- "Their home is gorgeous."
- "Did everyone bring their gloves?"
- "Someone left their wallet here."
- "I like shopping at the corner store because their staff is very helpful."

"There" is used when you're referring to a location. The location can be a physical place, or a place in a speech or action. Here are some examples of the correct use of the word "there."

- "The ball is over there."
- "The mountains over there are gorgeous."
- "There you are! I've been looking for you!"
- "She paused her monologue there until the laughter subsided."

5. "There's" versus "Theirs"

"There's" should only be used if the substitution of "there is" or "there has" would make sense.

Here are some examples of the correct use of "there's" as a substitute for "there is":

- "There's a huge funnel cloud forming in the north."
- "I don't want to bungee jump because there's a chance of getting hurt."

And here is an example of the correct use of "there's" as a substitute for "there has":

- "There's been a lot of stress in the workplace lately."

"Theirs" is a possessive pronoun. It is used to replace the combination of "their + noun." A noun is a person, place, or thing. Sorry, couldn't avoid a grammarian explanation for that one. Hopefully with some examples, this one will make sense.

"I saw that car in the driveway. Is it theirs?" could also be said like this:
"I saw that car in the driveway. Is it their car?" (car is a noun)

"I have a decent guitar, but theirs is better" could also be said like this: "I have a decent guitar, but their guitar is better." (guitar is a noun)

6. Missing Apostrophes

Apostrophes are easy to miss when you're racing to type up an article for a client, and are on a tight deadline. When you're proofreading your work, pay particular attention to words that should have an apostrophe (for example, contractions like shouldn't, can't, won't, et cetera) and add them in if they're missing.

7. Colon Mistakes

There are only two things that you need to remember about using colons within a sentence in your SEO articles.

First, whatever comes before the colon must be able to stand alone as a complete sentence.

Second, whatever comes after the colon should either explain that first sentence further, add to it in some way, or amplify it. The colon is a signal that what comes next is directly related to that first sentence.

WRONG
"I will teach you to: write in a style compatible with the needs of the SEO industry, find clients to write for, and earn decent rates for your work."

Note that "I will teach you to" is not a complete sentence on its own, therefore a colon after it is not appropriate.

CORRECT
"I will teach you how to do three things: write in a style compatible with the needs of the SEO industry, find clients to write for, and earn decent rates for your work."

In this case, "I will teach you how to do three things" could be a complete sentence on its own, and the content after the colon adds to that sentence.

Please note that the above rules only apply for the use of a colon in your sentences. There are also other uses for colons, which vary depending on which style guide you follow, for things such as citing references.

Also, if you want to use a colon in a headline or sub-headline, the first rule will not apply. For example, it would be perfectly acceptable to write the following headlines or sub-headlines in an SEO article:

- "Lions: The Scariest Mammal in the African Savannah"
- "Social Media: 3 Ways to Make it Work for You"

8. "Then" versus "Than"

Use "then" when discussing time. As in, "We had a Cub Scouts meeting, and then we went out for ice cream."

Include "than" in comparisons. "This party was more fun than the last one."

Bonus Tips

Here are a few more odds and ends (that your spell-checker won't catch!) to look for when you're proofreading your work:

- Using the wrong word (for example, writing "the" when you meant "then" or "right" when you meant "write")
- Missing words (for example, you wrote "Brush your teeth day" instead of "Brush your teeth every day"
- Double words (for example, you wrote "You should discuss

this <u>with with</u> him" instead of "You should discuss this with him")

- Make sure everything in your sentence is in a parallel form. I think of this as making sure that everything matches, or using the same pattern of words.
  - NOT SO GREAT: Being a good driver involves knowing how to focus, to pay attention to your surroundings, and that you always obey the traffic laws.
  - BETTER: Being a good driver involves know<u>ing</u> how to focus, pay<u>ing</u> attention to your surroundings, and obey<u>ing</u> the traffic laws.
  - For an excellent discussion of how to write in parallel form, with lots of examples, go to <u>https://owl.english.purdue.edu/owl/resource/623/01/</u>

Summing Up

Now that you know HOW to write good online content and avoid some of the more common pitfalls, you need to know how to turn your first draft into something that's free of errors (or pretty darned close!) Because the fastest way to lose a good client is to provide them with articles full of careless errors in spelling, grammar, and word usage.

The next chapter is going to show you effective ways of turning your first draft into a polished gem that your clients will love.

8 Steps to Producing Flawless Work That Impresses the Hell Out of Your Clients, and Keeps Them Coming Back for More!

"If we chase perfection we can catch excellence."
Vince Lombardi

Ok, I know… you're only human and humans are rarely flawless in anything they do.

But…

If you follow these tips correctly, your work will be truly excellent — and yes, you just might reach the level where you can say it's flawless.

And why will that impress the hell out of your clients? Because the odds are extremely high that they've hired freelance SEO writers in the past whose work is full of mistakes and requires heavy editing by the client themselves. Your work, on the other hand, gloriously free from errors (as close as humanly possible anyways!), will be a breath of fresh air to them. And they will LOVE you for it.

So let's get started now, shall we? Here are my eight steps to producing excellent work that impresses the hell out of your clients, and keeps them coming back for more!

1. Gather the Facts

The first step to producing an awesome article that your client will love is to gather the facts.

Research, my friend.

Open up your internet browser (for example, Chrome or Firefox), go to Google.com, and start searching for information on the topic of your article. Start taking point-form notes to collect as much useful information as you can. After you've collected enough intel on your topic, start to organize it into sub-categories.

For example, if you were writing an article titled "How to Get Rid of Wasps," you might divide your information into the following categories:

- Facts about wasps (intro)
- Steps to getting rid of wasps
- Precautions to take when getting rid of wasps

If you'll be including information in your article for which you need to give credit, be sure to make a list of references for your client. The easiest way to do this is to simply link to your information source within the article itself, using the the hyperlink feature of your word processor.

2. Think of a Catchy Headline (if your client hasn't already given you one to use!)

If your client hasn't already given you a headline for your article, then think of one yourself. Be sure to include the client's target keyword in your headline. For example, if the keyword you're targeting is "get rid of wasps," some headline options are:

- 10 Steps to Get Rid of Wasps in Your Yard
- How to Get Rid of Wasps Fast
- Pro Tips to Get Rid of Wasps Safely

3. Just Write. Then Save It… Twice.

Write the article, give it a quick read to make sure it flows and makes sense, then save it in two places. I recommend that you save one copy on your hard drive, and another on a USB stick for backup.

(Because let's face it, wouldn't it be a huge piss off to do all that hard work and then have your computer hard drive crash on you, meaning you'd have to re-write all of your articles? Back-up copies of your work are your new best friend!)

4. Leave it Alone for a Minimum of 24 Hours

After you've written that article and saved it in two places, leave it alone for a minimum of 24 hours before attempting to proofread it, if your deadline allows for this.

And preferably leave it alone for even longer than that.

In fact, whenever deadlines allow, I'll wait at least 48-72 hours before proofreading my own work.

The reason why you ought to wait a while before proofreading your own work is that we tend to be blind to our own errors. And the sooner we proofread our work after writing it, the more blind we are. Our brain is so efficient that it will correct many of the errors you've made as you read, so you won't even notice that they're there at all.

So say you wrote, "Choosing <u>then</u> right blinds for your living room makeover will have a huge impact on the end result."

The odds are high that if you proofread that sentence right after finishing it, your brain will auto-correct it and cause you to *think* you read, "Choosing <u>the</u> right blinds for your living room makeover will have a huge impact on the end result."

Sure, you could run your computer's spellcheck, but because the word "then" is correctly spelled, it won't pick up on the error. It's still an actual word, right?

So you, my friend, are the only one who can catch this.

On the one hand, it's all fine and dandy that our brains are trying to help us out by substituting the correct word as we read the error, but on the other hand, this "help" can really hinder our proofreading efforts.

Whenever possible, avoid proofreading your own work too soon after writing it. The longer the delay between writing and proofreading, the better!

5. Spellcheck is Free and Easy so USE IT

After your minimum 24 hours waiting period as described above, you're going to run your article through your computer's spellchecker.

Never, ever, neglect to use your word processor's spellcheck feature. This is one of the quickest tools you can use to remove the bulk of the mistakes in your work.

6. Proofread Your Article the Right Way

Proofreading isn't like regular reading where you sit back, relax, and let the words flow over you. Please don't do that — you'll miss too many errors.

Instead, you're going to read the article you wrote one word at a time, very slowly. Scrutinize every word to make sure it fits. Screen for the problems that I mention in the previous chapter on writing tips, and also be sure to look for the errors I mention in the upcoming chapter on common pitfalls.

Then read it again.

Take great care to read slowly, with no rush. You've got to be patient with this process, or you'll miss things. Many people find it helpful to do at least one proofread of their work out loud — there's something about speaking the words that makes certain kinds of errors jump off the page at you.

For example, if you were reading the following sentence out loud, the missing "n" in the word that should have been "then" practically screams at you.

"John tied his shoelaces, the went for a run."

However, if you were reading it silently, especially if you were rushing, your brain might have filled in the missing letter "n" for you, and you'd have thought it said, "John tied his shoelaces, then went for a run."

7. Use My Secret Weapon for a Final Check

My secret weapon to blast writing errors out of the water is Grammarly.com. They offer a free service that can catch many of the writing errors that your word processor's spelling and grammar check misses.

What kinds of errors does Grammarly catch?

They claim to be able to "instantly fix over 250 types of errors, most of which Microsoft Word can't find." This includes the kinds of errors that I go over in the previous chapter on writing pitfalls. For example, it can catch it if you use "its" when you should have used "it's." Or say you use the wrong verb tense, Grammarly can pick that up too! Pretty sweet if you ask me.

Now no piece of software is perfect, but the more tools you have at your disposal to catch errors in your work, the better.

Sometimes Grammarly will flag things as errors that are not wrong after all, and other times it misses stuff.

But, even if it catches only one or two genuine errors that you've missed, that's worth the few seconds of your time that it takes to run your work through this program. Because the fewer errors there are lying around for your client to find, the more work they'll send you and the better off you'll be.

Between your computer's spellchecker, Grammarly, and a careful proofread on your own, your writing should have little to no errors for your clients to find.

8. Provide Proof That Your Article is Unique and Not Plagiarized

Once you've gone through all five of the steps outlined above, run your article through Copyscape.com's Premium service. For five cents per article, they'll compare it to everything else that they can find published online. Any client who knows what they're doing will run your articles through this service before publishing them online anyways. So you might as well know what your client is going to find *before* you submit your article to them — this will give you an opportunity to fix any issues so that your client doesn't have to.

Now I know that you're going to be honest and make sure you don't commit plagiarism. But Copyscape has another use too.

What if some of the wording that you came up with on your own is the same as what someone else has already published online? Not only could this make it appear as if you copied them (which could reflect badly on you), but it will also count as duplicate content online (which your client will not want).

Your client needs SEO articles that the search engines consider unique, since unique articles have better odds of ranking well in the search engines. So my advice to you is that if Copyscape finds any phrasing in your article that matches what has already been published elsewhere, you change your word choices until Copyscape no longer pulls up a match.

Summing Up

If you take care to avoid the more common writing pitfalls, write in a style that's well-suited to online readers, and follow the steps in this chapter to eliminate errors, you'll end up with work that's much better than the vast majority of your competition.

How do I know this?

Because I've hired writers to take some of the load off me when I wanted a break from writing, but still needed to produce content to keep my clients happy. And let me tell you, most people who apply for my writing jobs can't hack it.

But you, dear reader, now know the secrets to making your writing shine brightly in a sea of mediocrity. And that will set you apart from the herd.

Now that you know how to do *that*, it's time to learn how to set up your business. The next chapter contains a blueprint for setting up your SEO writing business within a week. Let's get to it!

How to Set Up Your Business Within a Week (Even if You're Not a Techie!)

"The best time to plant a tree was 20 years ago. The second best time is now." Chinese Proverb

I don't want you to feel overwhelmed at the thought of starting a freelance SEO-writing business.

This chapter will help you to avoid that — it contains an easy-to-follow blueprint to getting started. And the good news is, it's totally doable within a week. But don't worry, that doesn't mean you *have* to do it all in a week. You can stretch it out longer if you want. Or, if you have extra time on your hands, you may even be able to set everything up in less than a week. It's all up to you!

Are you ready? Then let's get started!

Days 1 and 2

First, ensure that you have a reliable computer or laptop with a word-processing program.

It really doesn't matter what kind of computer or laptop you use. As long as it's reliable and has a program on it that you can use to write your articles in, you're good to go. I use <u>OpenOffice</u>, which is totally free. Another popular program is Microsoft Word, although that'll cost you.

If you don't already have a computer or laptop, then head to the mall today and check out the prices. There will be lots to choose from so it shouldn't be hard to find one that suits your budget.

Second, sign up for high-speed internet service.

As for the internet, odds are you have access to a wide range of services and internet speeds. To maximize your hourly earning potential, I recommend that you go with an internet service that is capable of loading the average webpage in five seconds or less.

This is not the time to be cheap and get dial-up internet. Trust me, if you do that, your hourly wage will plummet since you'll be wasting a ridiculous amount of time watching your computer load webpages so slowly that it will pain you to watch.

You see, when you're researching your SEO articles, you'll be doing your research online. Say you need to gather information from 20 or more different webpages, and they each take 30 seconds to load on your screen. That would mean you'd waste 10 minutes just loading the webpages you need to see for research purposes, never mind the time it takes you to actually read them, plus outline and write your article. Whereas if those same webpages take only two seconds each to load, you'll have all the research information you need in front of you in less than a minute.

Now imagine that you're writing eight articles per day, and need to view 160 pages during your research (eight articles x 20 webpages each for research). With slow speed internet taking 10 seconds per page to load, that's one hour and 20 minutes every single day that you're going to spend just staring at your computer screen doing nothing but waiting… and waiting some more. Trust me, I've been there (not by choice) and it's painful.

On the other hand, if those same pages can load in two seconds each, that's less than six minutes per day spent waiting. Or, at five seconds to load per research page, you'd spend just under 14 minutes per day in total waiting.

Additionally, when you submit your work to your client, you'll have to upload your articles to your e-mail provider as attachments. Upload speeds are almost always much slower than download speeds, so once again, don't cheap out on your internet service by signing up for something ridiculously slow like dial-up internet — instead, purchase a reliable high-speed internet package that will allow you to upload your work to your client quickly and easily.

If you don't already have high-speed internet, call the internet provider of your choice today and sign up for new service (or upgrade your existing service if necessary). Sometimes it takes a few days for them to set you up, so it's best to do this now.

Third, set up a way to get paid.

Most clients, and many freelancing websites, will already be using PayPal to get money to their freelancers. So, if you don't already have a PayPal account, I recommend that you sign up for one now. It's better to have this set up ahead of time rather than futz around with trying to figure it out on the fly when you start landing clients.

You can sign up for a PayPal account here: https://www.paypal.com/

PayPal is easy to set up, and easy to use. They are capable of handling many different currencies (24, at the time of this writing) from countries around the world — this comes in handy if you find yourself doing work for someone outside of your home country.

Remember, quality content that's written in English is required around the world. I've written for clients in Canada, the United States, the UK, and India — and you could too!

Days 3 and 4

Write three or four sample articles.

It's pretty much a guarantee that potential clients will want to see samples of your work before they hire you. I recommend that you put together three or four sample articles on unrelated topics (to add diversity to your profile and show that you can write about a wide range of subject matter). To make the process of writing your sample articles as easy as possible, try to choose topics that you are already very familiar with and will require little to no research.

Here are some ideas to get you started:

- If you've ever re-painted a room in your house and it turned out amazing, write a how-to article on how to paint like a pro.
- If you're a master of BBQ cooking, write an article on how to get great results from cooking on the BBQ.
- If you're great at de-cluttering your home, write an article on quick and easy ways to declutter your home.
- If you have the greenest, healthiest lawn on the block, write an article on how to make your lawn the envy of the neighborhood.

I bet you'll be able to think of tons of things to write about for your sample articles now. Take some time right now to write out a list of ideas. There are lots of things that you can write about that won't require you to put in a bunch of time researching the topic.

Or, save time and look over my free list of 81 topic ideas. (You can get it if you <u>sign up for the Money Machine Inner Circle</u> — membership is free!) Not only will it save you time coming up with topic ideas, but it'll show you headline formats that are popular for online content (and the fact that your article headlines are well-suited to online content will impress potential clients, making it more likely that they'll hire you.)

Now, your mileage may vary, but I find that writing my articles goes a lot faster if I write a point-form outline first.

A sample article should be 500-600 words long, and revolve around a keyword phrase. I don't recommend that you write a longer article than that since your potential clients probably won't have time to read it if it goes on and on.

Here is a sample outline for an article targeting the keyword, "Get Rid of Raccoons."

Headline: How to Get Rid of Raccoons

Intro… 2-3 sentences

Sub-headline: Get Rid of Raccoons By Making Your Property Unattractive to Them

-Properly secured waste containers
-Don't leave bowls of pet food outdoors
-Etc.

Sub-headline: Seal Off Raccoon Entry Points

-Attics
-Foundations
-Sheds
-What to look for, how to do this humanely

Sub-headline: Precautions When Trying to Get Rid of Raccoons

-Rabies
-Baby raccoons, mating season, importance
-Wildlife protection laws that apply to raccoons

Sub-headline: Learning How to Get Rid of Raccoons is Easy

-Concluding paragraph, 2-4 sentences that sum up the entire article

Once you have your outline written out, it's quick and easy to fill in the blanks. Make sure that you use your keyword in the article's headline, and also within the sub-headlines, if it fits naturally. For a 500-600 word article, remember to try to include the exact keyword phrase about four times:

- once in the headline
- once in the first sentence
- in two or three of the sub-headlines; ideally, spread out naturally between the beginning and end of the article.

Use the above template only as a guide for keyword usage. Your clients may want you to use the keyword more, or less, often — just follow their lead and you'll be fine.

Also remember that it's important for you to use the keyword in a way that flows as naturally as possible. You want to do it in such a manner that the average reader won't even notice that you're doing it.

Try to write a couple of articles on day three, and two more on day four. Boom! Your samples are done. You can come back to them in a couple of days and proofread them.

Day 5

Make a list of potential clients.

The easiest, least intimidating way to get started for a beginner is to write for a web content agency.

You can find these companies by doing a quick Google search, or, you could set up a profile on a freelancer website such as UpWork.com and look for work there.

Here is one web content agency that I found via a Google search: http://needanarticle.com.

Another option is this one: http://www.writeraccess.com/.

Lastly, if you're already a fairly skilled writer, you could try an agency that offers work at higher rates, such as this one: http://articlebunny.com/.

Note: I am not endorsing any of those agencies — they're just meant as an example of the kind of agency you could write for.

Writing agencies like the ones listed above hire writers to provide content for publishing online. All of your work will likely be ghostwritten. The nice thing about working for an agency like this is that you're likely to have steady work, and you don't need to juggle a bunch of clients with separate deadlines all on your own.

A typical scenario goes something like this…

The agency will give you access to a spreadsheet listing all of the articles they need written, along with the deadlines for each. You choose as many as you want to write.

So say life is busy right now and all you can handle is a couple of articles a week? Odds are, they'll be fine with that. Or maybe you want to make a lot of quick cash — in that case, you'll be able to choose a larger number of articles that week and make a lot more money.

I think that working for a web content agency is a great way to get your feet wet and build your confidence. It's a quick way of proving to yourself that you are capable of being paid for, and pleasing your client with, your writing.

A peek into the future...

Once you've built up your confidence and skills, it'll be time to go where the real money is.

You're going to cut out the middle man and work directly with clients. There is a lot more money to be made here since you get to pocket ALL the cash being charged for an article, rather than losing a percentage of it to an agency. This is how I was able to make as much as $60 an hour for my time.

The kinds of clients that you can work for include SEO Agencies (companies that help websites to rank more highly in the search engine results), and small businesses who want to maintain an active blog but don't have the time to write all that content. I know of a guy who managed to land $3000 worth of work in a month from a single small business owner after spending some time pitching to a bunch of them that had inactive blogs!

Because you're cutting out one of the middle men by working directly with an SEO agency or small business, you can make more money per article. However, you'll be the one who is responsible for finding enough clients to meet your income goals.

How do you get work directly from SEO Agencies and small businesses?

One way to do it is to simply Google "SEO company" and make a list of prospects. You can either e-mail them directly or use the "Contact Us" form on their website to pitch your writing services.

Day 6

Set up an e-mail that you will use for your SEO writing business.

There are lots of free e-mail services that you can use for your freelance SEO writing business. Don't bother paying for a fancy schmancy paid service — it's simply not necessary, and your money can be better spent on other aspects of your business at this point.

I recommend that you use a web-based free service such as Gmail.

Make your business e-mail address sound professional — do not make the mistake of choosing a cute name like SweetMelissa@gmail.com or HotBob@gmail.com.

Instead, use something like YourNameFreelanceSEO@gmail.com or YourNameProSEO@gmail.com.

You'll be using this e-mail address to reply to client inquiries, and/or to pitch your services to new potential clients.

Day 7

Proofread your sample articles.

This one is simple: Follow the steps in the previous chapter on how to produce flawless work and you'll be all set.

You're Done!

Pat yourself on the back because you've finished up with everything you needed to do to set up your new business.

Coming up next is an optional step. I've seen people succeed without it; however, if you have the time, I highly recommend that you take this extra step in order to increase the professional appearance of your business — this can make it easier to land clients.

(Optional, But Highly Recommended) Set Up a Self-Hosted WordPress Site

If done right, a self-hosted WordPress site can act as your online business card for your freelance SEO writing services. You can refer potential clients to it for a listing of your services and rates, plus to see your writing samples and client testimonials.

Details on how to set up a self-hosted Wordpress site are beyond the scope of this book, but it's easy to do. In a nutshell, all you do is purchase a domain name, purchase web hosting, install Wordpress on your site, and customize it the way you want it.

If you are interested in setting up your own website for your business, sign up for the Money Machine Inner Circle for FREE at http://averybreyer.com/money-machine-book-opt-in1/, and you'll get instant access to a free report listing exactly which services I recommend for setting up your site. Especially if you're new to the world of setting up a website, this will save you a ton of time since you won't have to waste time researching which services are the best or easiest to use for a non-techie.

A basic website should have the following pages:

Home Page

This is where you describe your freelance SEO writing services, and even include a testimonial or two once you've worked with clients for a while.

Samples Page

Use this page to show off the sample articles that you've written.

About Page

This is where you explain who you are, your experience (if any), and why someone should hire you.

Contact Page

This is where you set up a simple contact form that visitors to your website can use to get in touch with you.

Action Steps

1. On days 1 and 2, make sure you have a reliable computer, access to high-speed internet, and a PayPal account set up. If you don't have these things, be sure to get them!

2. On days 3 and 4, choose topics for your sample articles and write them up. Aim for 500-600 words per article.

3. On day 5, make a list of potential clients.

4. On day 6, set up an e-mail address that you'll use for your online writing business.

5. On day 7, proofread your sample articles from days 3 and 4.

6. (Optional Step) If you want to set up your own website to advertise your services, you can either squeeze this in over the previous week, or work on it gradually over the next while.

Summing Up

Now that you know all of the steps required to set up your freelance SEO-writing business, it's almost time to hit the ground running and execute the plan. Because if you don't take action, you won't get results, right?

But before you do, read the next chapter. It contains important information on persistence, plus goes over the most common hurdles that new SEO writers face (and how to deal with them). Because the last thing I want is for you to get started on this new venture and get stuck. So keep reading…

The Importance of Persistence

"Everybody has a plan until they get punched in the mouth." Mike Tyson

The ability to persist in the face of adversity is one of the key differences between those who succeed at earning extra cash by becoming a freelance SEO writer, and those who don't.

And you're going to be one of the ones who succeeds, right?

If you want to earn money as a successful freelance SEO writer, you need to be prepared for adversity. You need to decide right now that you're going to rise above it. Because no matter how well you prepare, no matter how much experience you end up having, there will always be bumps in the road to success.

And nothing worth succeeding at comes without effort.

Problems You May Run Into and How to

Handle Them

Here are some of the most common problems that new SEO writers run into, and how to handle them in a way that makes you stronger and wiser for the experience.

You may have a string of wins, and then out of blue, BOOM! A client doesn't pay you, despite the fact that you've asked several times.

If you've taken all reasonable measures to get paid, and the client is being a jerk, then it's time to cut the cord and move on. You'll find a better client to replace the bad apple. If you follow the guidance in the previous chapter on how to find great clients, the vast majority of your clients will be fantastic and WANT to pay you. Why? Because you do good work that they <u>need</u> help with, and paying you is the only way that they can guarantee that you'll continue to do so.

You've applied for several SEO writing jobs, or sent out several e-mails to offer your services and no-one has hired you?

Remind yourself that "All it takes is one!" Because you only need one good client to kick your new SEO writing business off to a profitable start.

But while you're waiting to land that first job, use this as an opportunity to review the text of the e-mail inquiries that you're sending to potential clients. Fiddle with the e-mail a bit — change the wording, or add some personality to make yourself stand out from the pile of utterly boring, ho-hum e-mails they get every day.

Also, in the beginning stages of your business, don't focus on how many clients you're landing — instead, focus on how many potential clients you're pitching to each day. Because the law of averages is in your favor here — if you contact enough people, eventually, you'll find someone who needs your services and is willing to pay for them.

And once you've landed your first clients, you can ask for testimonials from them, which will make it even easier to land the next one.

Your client found a bunch of typos in the article you sent them?

Whatever you do, don't beat yourself up — you're only human after all and it's normal to make mistakes, especially in the early stages of your business. Wipe the egg off your face, learn from your mistakes, fix the typos, then do better next time.

You feel weird about sending e-mails to potential clients and worry that you're bothering them?

Repeat after me my friend: "I am offering them an extremely valuable service that their company can benefit from, and am doing them a FAVOR by letting them know how I can help."

If you don't let them know that you can help them out, how on earth are they going to find you? And the thing about sending out an e-mail is that you'll be competing for work with no-one other than yourself — this is so much easier than competing with tons of other applicants to a formal job posting.

Keep Your Eye on the Prize

You'll have a much easier time overcoming any obstacles in your path to earning money as a successful freelance SEO writer if you have a clear idea of the benefits that you'll get from doing all this work.

Take a few moments and imagine how freelance SEO writing could improve your life...

How will the money earned from this venture help you? Will you use it for small luxuries that you couldn't afford before? Will you save the money for a big purchase down the road? Will you use it to pay off your debt?

How will having full control over where and when you work improve your life?

The Snowball Effect

Once you start to get some small successes, you'll see that it becomes easier to succeed the next time. Your successes will start to snowball, getting bigger and bigger the more you push yourself!

For example, let's say you do a really great job for a client. You could ask them for a testimonial, which you can then use as proof of your skills, making it easier to land the next client.

Or how about your hourly earnings — your persistence in honing your skills and becoming more efficient can lead to your earnings starting to snowball too. In the beginning, it might take you an hour, or even two, to write a $20 article. But you're going to become a faster researcher and typist the more you practice. Six months from now, you could be writing three of those articles per hour, making $60 an hour for your time.

As with most things in life, your persistence *will* pay off if you keep at it long enough.

Summing Up

Now that you know about some of the more common hurdles that you might face as a new SEO writer, and more importantly, how to deal with them, you're ready to go!

You've learned about a method of earning money that most people have never heard of, that doesn't have a lot of REAL competition, and can earn you very good money for your time.

This is the very same path that I followed to earn up to $60 per hour of my time, to turn my computer into a money machine — with no prior experience, no fancy degree in journalism or writing, and no connections.

If doing the same appeals to you, be sure to sign up for free membership in the Money Machine Inner Circle. You'll get instant access to a series of exclusive FREE bonuses:

- A list of the exact tools I use every day (most of which are free to use), which will help you to produce better work (and THAT tends to lead to getting paid more!)
- A list of the exact services that I used to set up my freelance writing website quickly and easily, even though I'm not a techie! This is the list I wish I'd had when I set up my first website since it would have saved me a ton of research time — and now it's yours!
- A list of 81 topic ideas for your sample articles — this will give you an idea of the kinds of topics that are suitable for samples and the headline formats that tend to get more attention. It's a must-have for anyone who is new to this business!
- Last, but not least, if I ever come across any other info that I think will be of use to you, your membership in the Inner Circle will allow me to get it to you quickly and easily

Sign up now at the link below, before you forget!

http://averybreyer.com/money-machine-book-opt-in1/

Did You Enjoy This Book?

I want to thank you for purchasing and reading this book. I really hope you got a lot out of it!

Can I ask you for a quick favor though?

If you enjoyed this book, I would really appreciate it if you could leave me a review on Amazon.

I love getting feedback from my readers, and reviews on Amazon really do make a difference. I read all of my reviews and would love to hear your thoughts.

Thanks so much!

Avery Breyer

P.S. You can use the link below to go directly to the book on Amazon and leave your review.

http://www.amazon.com/dp/B0185Z29LY

More Books by Avery Breyer

How to Stop Living Paycheck to Paycheck

In this best-selling budgeting bible, you'll get the motivation and know-how to build up a big stash of emergency cash, get rid of debt, make sure you never run out of money, and avoid the 11 worst budget traps (that will ruin your financial plans if you let them!)

http://www.amazon.com/dp/B00UVSHAWM/

How to Raise Your Credit Score

Find out how to pump up your credit score and be approved for credit cards, loans, and mortgages with ease, plus, save money with the lowest interest rates that are only offered to the financial first class!

http://www.amazon.com/dp/B00Y2OR2H4/

34589727R00047

Made in the USA
San Bernardino, CA
02 June 2016